Dear Parent:
Your child's love of reading starts here!

Every child learns to read in a diffe ... n speed. Some go back and forth bet ... favorite books again and again. Ot ... n order. You can help your young reader ... ore confident by encouraging his or her own interests and ab... . From books your child reads with you to the first books he or she reads alone, there are I Can Read Books for every stage of reading:

SHARED READING
Basic language, word repetition, and whimsical illustrations, ideal for sharing with your emergent reader

BEGINNING READING
Short sentences, familiar words, and simple concepts for children eager to read on their own

READING WITH HELP
Engaging stories, longer sentences, and language play for developing readers

READING ALONE
Complex plots, challenging vocabulary, and high-interest topics for the independent reader

ADVANCED READING
Short paragraphs, chapters, and exciting themes for the perfect bridge to chapter books

I Can Read Books have introduced children to the joy of reading since 1957. Featuring award-winning authors and illustrators and a fabulous cast of beloved characters, I Can Read Books set the standard for beginning readers.

A lifetime of discovery begins with the magical words "I Can Read!"

Visit www.icanread.com for information
on enriching your child's reading experience.

For Scarlet
—R.S.

I Can Read Book® is a trademark of HarperCollins Publishers.

Splat the Cat: Blow, Snow, Blow
Copyright © 2013 by Rob Scotton
All rights reserved. Manufactured in China.
No part of this book may be used or reproduced in any manner whatsoever without written permission except in the case of brief quotations embodied in critical articles and reviews. For information address HarperCollins Children's Books, a division of HarperCollins Publishers, 195 Broadway, New York, NY 10007.
www.icanread.com

Library of Congress catalog card number: 2013936888
ISBN 978-0-06-209026-3 (trade bdg.) —ISBN 978-0-06-209027-0 (pbk.)

14 15 16 SCP 10 9 8 7 6 5 4 3 2 ❖ First Edition

Splat the Cat
Blow, Snow, Blow

Based on the bestselling books by Rob Scotton

Cover art by Rick Farley

Text by Amy Hsu Lin

Interior illustrations by Robert Eberz

HARPER
An Imprint of HarperCollinsPublishers

Splat stared out the window.

"When will it snow?" he asked Mom.

He wanted to make a snowcat,

the biggest and best snowcat ever!

"Try to let it go, Splat," said Mom.

"Don't worry. It will snow," said Dad.

"You said that a long time ago," said Splat.

Splat looked to and fro.

Wait, was that snow?

No . . .

"This snow is too slow," said Splat.

"When will it show?"

Then Splat said, "I know!

I'll grow my own snow!"

"Snow is wet and cold," said Splat.

So he got some ice and put it in a bowl.

Then Splat said,

"Snow is light and white."

So he shook out his pillow.

Next Splat said,

"Now I need a little wind to blow."

Splat forgot to set the fan on low.

It made the bowl overflow.

"Oh no!" said Splat.

Little Sis shook her head.

She said, "Don't you know?

You can't grow snow."

15

As Splat cleaned up the mess,

he started feeling low.

"When will it ever snow?" he said.

"I know!" said Splat. "I'll think snow!"

Splat put on his yellow snowsuit.

Then Splat took out his sled

and put all his ducks in a row.

"We're ready to go," Splat said.

"Blow, snow, blow!"

He waited.

And waited.

And lo and behold,

it began to snow!

But the snow was just so-so.

It was very, very slow.

Splat said, "This snow is too low
for the sled to go,
but I can still make a snowcat."
Splat got a wheelbarrow.
He dumped the snow
to start making a cat.

"What is that?" Little Sis asked.

"A snowcat," said Splat.

Little Sis added a bow.

She said, "Now it's

a snowy little kitten like me!"

25

Splat and Little Sis tried

to play catch in the snow,

but there wasn't enough to throw,

and the light was getting low.

26

"Time for dinner!" called Dad.

Everyone sat down to eat,

but Splat could barely swallow.

He kept looking out the window.

Then the wind started to blow.

The low snow began to grow . . .

and grow . . .

and grow!

Splat and his family stayed cozy.

They roasted marshmallows

by the fire's glow.

They made shadow shapes

and told silly stories.

The next morning, Splat saw
loads of snow!
Splat built the best snowcat ever.